Turbulent
Planet

Crumbling Earth
Erosion & Landslides

Mary Colson

Chicago, Illinois

For information, address the publisher:
Raintree, 100 N. LaSalle, Suite 1200, Chicago, IL 60602
Color Reproduction by Dot Gradations Ltd, UK
Printed and bound in China
10 09 08 07 06
10 9 8 7 6 5 4 3 2 1

Library of Congress Cataloging-in-Publication Data

Colson, Mary.
 Crumbling earth erosion and landslides / Mary Colson.
  p. cm. -- (Turbulent planet)
 Includes bibliographical references and index.
 ISBN 1-4109-1741-X (lib. bdg.) -- ISBN 1-4109-1751-7 (pbk.)
 1. Geodynamics--Juvenile literature.
 2. Erosion--Juvenile literature. 3. Geology, Structural--Juvenile literature. [1. Erosion. 2. Geodynamics.
 3. Geology.] I. Title. II. Series. QE501.25.C66 2005
 551.3--dc22
                                             2005004231

This leveled text is a version of Freestyle: Turbulent Planet: Crumbling Earth.

Acknowledgments

p.4/5, PA Photos/EPA; p.4, Popperfoto; p.5 bottom, FLPA/D Fleetham, Silvestris; p.5 middle, PA Photos/EPA; p.5 top, Oxford Scientific Films/T. C. Middleton; p.6, FLPA/Silvestris Fotoservice; p.6/7, Getty Images Imagebank; p.7, Oxford Scientific Films/Roland Mayr; p.9, NASA; p.10/11, Oxford Scientific Films/John Downer; p.10, Rex Features; p.11, FLPA/USDA; p.12/13, Corbis/Lloyd Cluff; p.12, Corbis; p.13, Corbis/Bettmann; p.14/15, PA Photos/EPA; p.14, Oxford Scientific Films/David Tipling; p.15, Oxford Scientific Films/Alastair Shay; p.16/17, Corbis; p.16, FLPA/Mark Newman; p.17, Corbis; p.18/19, Corbis/Jonathan Blair; p.18, OSF/Kynan Bazley; p.19, Science Photo Library/NASA; p.20/21, Corbis/Ron Watts; p.20, PA Photos/Martin Keene; p.21, Alamy/Worldwide Picture Library; p.22, PA Photos/Chris Ison; p.23, Associated Press; p.24/25, Skyscan; p.24, Corbis/Elio Ciol; p.25, Corbis/James L. Amos; p.26/27, Magnum Photos; p.26, Oxford Scientific Films/T. C. Middleton; p.27, Corbis/Kim Kulish, Saba; p.28/29, Corbis; p.29 right, NASA Goddard Laboratory for Atmospheres/Hasler, Peirce, Palaniappan, Manyin; p.30/31, Corbis/Annie Griffiths Belt; p.30, Associated Press; p.32/33, Corbis/Bob Gomel; p.33, Corbis/David Butow; p.34/35, Oxford Scientific Films/Richard Packwood; p.34, Oxford Scientific Films/Keren Su; p.35, Oxford Scientific Films/Andrew Park, SAL; p.36/37, Corbis; p.36, FLPA/Wendy Dennis; p.37, Rex Features; p.38/39, Corbis/Galen Rowell; p.38, Oxford Scientific Films/Stan Osolinski; p.39, FLPA/D Fleetham, Silvestris; p.40/41, FLPA/E. & D. Hosking; p.40, Naturepl/Martha Holmes; p.42 left, Ecoscene/Tony Page; p.42 right, Ecoscene/Andy Rockall; p.43, Associated Press; p.45, Corbis/Lloyd Cluff

Cover photograph reproduced with permission of Corbis

Every effort has been made to contact copyright holders of any material reproduced in this book. Any omissions will be rectified in subsequent printings if notice is given to the Publishers.

Contents

Any words appearing in the text in bold, **like this**, are explained in the Glossary. You can also look out for some of them in the Wild Words box at the bottom of each page.

Shaking and Sliding

△ Landslides can cause terrible damage.

What would happen if the ground under your feet started to shake? Imagine how it would feel. You cannot keep your balance. Everything is rattling and falling. The walls of your home are moving back and forth.

Moving ground

You take a look outside. The hillside is moving. Soil and rocks are falling down the hill and toward your town. It is a **landslide**. Nothing can stop it. As the land moves downhill, it picks up more dirt and rocks.

Buried

The landslide gets bigger and faster. More soil and mud rush down. Rocks crush the buildings and vehicles in their paths. The landslide blocks roads and buries homes.

Everyone tries to escape from the landslide. But there is nowhere to go. People are looking for each other. They start to dig in the dirt. They are searching for lost family members.

Find out later . . .

. . . how this rock got its shape.

. . . what makes landslides happen.

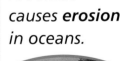

. . . what causes **erosion** in oceans.

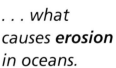

erosion   wearing away by wind, water, ice, or other forces

5

Changing World

New shapes
Sometimes hot, liquid rock bursts through Earth's surface. When the rock cools and hardens, new areas of land, like those below, are formed.

A **landslide** happens when huge masses of land slip down mountains or over cliffs. Often the rocks and dirt come down in a sudden rush. This is called an **avalanche**.

Avalanches are made of snow and ice mixed with rocks, soil, and mud. Avalanches and landslides can quickly change Earth's surface.

Slow changes
Other, slower, processes also change Earth's surface. These changes are happening all the time. They can take thousands of years.

Wild Words avalanche quickly falling mass of snow, ice, rocks, or mud

Erupting volcanoes

Plate movements also cause **volcanoes** to form. Some form in oceans where plates are moving apart. Melted rock from below pushes up through the crust. It piles up on the seabed forming volcanic mountains.

In other places, one plate is pushed under another. Melted rock then rises to form volcanoes. Hot **gases** and liquid rock called **lava** flow from volcanoes.

Volcano in Washington

Mount St. Helens (below) in the state of Washington **erupted** in 1980. The erupting volcano caused an **avalanche** of rock and mud.

These mountains formed when volcanoes erupted on the edge of the African plate.

Shaping the Planet

Burning city
After an earthquake in 1906, San Francisco (below) burned for three days.

Many natural forces help to shape or damage our **environment**.

After the quake

As we have seen, an **earthquake** is a shaking of the Earth's **crust**. Very often, the real damage happens after the quaking stops. Buildings that are shaken can give way later without warning. **Gas** pipes can break and start fires.

At the San Andreas **Fault** in California the Pacific and North American **plates** are slowly pushing past each other. The area gets many, mostly small earthquakes every year. ▷

Earthquake damage

Earthquakes can start **landslides** and **floods**. They can also cause **volcanoes** to **erupt** and spark fires.

Killer waves

Earthquakes can also set off big ripples across the surface of the oceans. The ripples make huge waves named **tsunamis**. Along coasts the waves can be over 100 feet (30 meters) high. Tsunamis move across the ocean at 470 miles (750 kilometers) per hour. The huge rush of water damages coastline rock and washes away soil.

On December 26, 2004 an undersea earthquake in the Indian Ocean caused a tsunami. Over 300,000 people were killed.

The longest earthquake

One of the longest recorded earthquakes was in Alaska in 1964. It lasted four minutes. About 30 city blocks were damaged, like the one below.

fault   crack or fracture in Earth's crust

Kinds of erosion

Natural **erosion** makes changes over long periods of time. Erosion by wind and water can change the shape of rocks and create caves. These changes are often extremely slow. We may not even notice the changes in our lifetimes.

Landslides change the landscape much more quickly. They can cause terrible damage. Many people have died or lost their homes in landslides.

Carving blocks

This area in Ireland is a **limestone** pavement. The surface of the limestone has been **dissolved** by water into separate blocks.

Heavy rain caused a ▷ landslide in Honduras, South America, in 1998. Over 500,000 people lost their homes.

Loose soil

Landslides start for all kinds of reasons. **Earthquakes**, heavy rains, and **volcanoes** can all cause landslides. Soil needs the roots of trees or other **vegetation** to hold it together. If people cut down forests, soil and rocks will slip or get washed away.

Creating caves

This cave system in Malaysia was formed by water erosion. It contains the biggest cave in the world.

vegetation   living plants, including trees

New land

Rocks are sometimes formed on the seabed. Earth movements lift them up to form new land. These land areas are then worn away. New natural wonders are created.

Uluru

Uluru, or Ayers Rock, in central Australia is an enormous, isolated rock. It stands in a desert that was once an ocean. Sand piled up on the ocean floor, creating this huge, hard rock.

The land around Uluru was once as high as the rock itself. It has been worn away over millions of years. ▽

"The Wave"

This cliff in Australia was **eroded** by wind and rain into a wave shape.

Victoria Falls

Along the Zambezi River in Africa, the ground and water make a sudden, deep drop. The drop has created one of the greatest waterfalls in the world, Victoria Falls. The river plunges into a deep **rift valley** that crosses its path. The valley was formed by movements in Earth's **crust**.

High falls

Victoria Falls (above) on the Zambezi River in Africa is over 355 feet (108 meters) high.

rift valley   valley formed when a block of land slips down
               between faults

Ice and Water

Water and ice have been shaping and **eroding** Earth's surface for millions of years.

Expanding ice

One way water erodes rock is by freezing. Water takes up more space when it turns to ice. When water is trapped in rock and turns to ice, it **expands**. This can crack the rock. The water then freezes deeper inside the rock. In time the rock erodes away.

Glaciers

Glaciers are rivers of ice that carve their way through land. Usually they move very slowly.

Avalanches

An **avalanche** of snow and ice, like the one below, can erode rocks. Avalanches usually happen without any warning.

Wild Words   expand   get bigger

Over time, glaciers wear away the rock in their paths. They have shaped bays in Europe. They have carved valleys and mountains in South America, Alaska, and Asia.

Lambert Glacier
Below is a view from the air of the Lambert Glacier in **Antarctica**. It is at least one and a half times the size of Texas. That makes it the world's largest glacier.

◁   Glaciers look like big, white highways or rivers. This glacier is over 36 miles (58 kilometers) long.

glacier   slow-moving river of ice

Carving a path

Rivers are one of the main forces that shape our landscape. They carry rocks and soil that wear away **riverbeds**. The Colorado River is hundreds of miles long. Over time it has **eroded** deserts and mountains to make a passage through the land. It has even carved out the Grand **Canyon**.

The Colorado River winds through the Grand Canyon for over 277 miles (445 kilometers). ▽

Passing through

Katherine **Gorge** (above) in Australia was formed by the river that passes through it. Over many years, the river created the steep sides of the gorge by wearing away rock.

Wild Words   gorge   narrow valley between hills or mountains

Raining on rocks

It is not just the river's water that has shaped the Grand Canyon. Rain and ice have played their parts, too. The land in the Grand Canyon is hard and dry. It only rains a few times a year. The hard ground cannot **absorb** the rain. The rain pours into the canyon. It carries loose rocks with it.

In the winter rainwater can freeze in the rocks. As the ice **expands**, it cracks and loosens the rocks.

The Amazon River

The Amazon River (below) has carved a path through six countries in South America.

absorb   soak up

Flood danger

When the water level in a river rises, there may be a danger of **floods**. If a river breaks its banks, water can flood the land very suddenly. Floods **erode** farmland by washing away the soil. They can also wash away food crops.

In 1997 the Yangtze River in China flooded. The floods washed away rice and wheat crops. Many thousands of people faced **starvation**.

Low land alongside a wide river can flood easily. ▽

Wild Words   starvation   extreme lack of food or death from hunger

Storms in Mozambique

In the year 2000, **tropical** storms hit Mozambique in Africa. The storm rains filled the rivers. The rivers overflowed. There were three weeks of flooding. Over half a million people had to leave their homes. Roads, bridges, and farms were destroyed.

Flood facts

- Flood damage in the United States costs more than $3 billion every year.

- Around the world thousands of people die every year because of flooding.

A helicopter rescued these flood victims from a rooftop in Mozambique.

▽

tropical   having to do with or coming from the tropics, which is
          the region of Earth either side of the equator

Ocean erosion

The ocean causes great **erosion** along coastlines. Storm waves pick up loose rocks and **gravel** and hurl them at the shore. The waves wear away the land.

Wave power

Waves can make cliffs collapse and beaches disappear. They can also carve rocks into great shapes like these (below) at Étretat in France.

△ Most of Hallsands in Great Britain was washed away when the ocean eroded the shore.

Wild Words gravel mixture of sand and small stones

Washed away

Sometimes people help speed up erosion. There was once a **shingle** beach close to a town in Great Britain. The shingle was taken away. There was nothing to protect the town and land from the waves. The land **eroded** quickly. In 1917 a storm washed most of the town away.

New sand

New sand has been added to this beach in South Carolina (below). It replaces the sand that the ocean has swept away.

shingle   mass of small rocks on the shore of an ocean or lake

Wind and Weathering

Red rocks

There are more than 2,000 **limestone** arches in Arches National Park, Utah (below). The rocks there have been eroded by sand and dirt blown by the wind.

The weather plays an important part in changing Earth's surface. Rain, sun, and wind can do a lot of damage to the landscape. This kind of damage is known as **weathering**.

Effects of weather

Different kinds of weather act in different ways. Wind **erosion** occurs when strong winds pick up sand and dirt and blow them away. The sand and dirt carried by the wind can **erode** rocks. It wears them away like sandpaper. Rain washes away **nutrients** in the soil.

A long period without rain is a **drought**. In Ethiopia in Africa, even the trees cannot survive the drought.

Dry land

Too much sunshine makes the ground dry. Ponds, rivers, and streams dry up. If there is no rainfall, the land gets too dry for plants to grow. Even if it does rain, the water cannot soak into the hard, dry land. Instead, it flows across the surface and washes away the soil.

Ruined homes

A **landslide** wrecked these houses in California (above). The landslide was caused by a storm.

Stormy weather

Damage caused by weather is not always slow. Powerful winds can change the land in seconds. They can destroy forests. Wind can also crumple strong buildings and rip off roofs.

Spinning winds

A **cyclone** is a system of spinning winds. There are different types of cyclone. One kind that causes a lot of damage is a **hurricane**.

Tornado trouble

A **tornado** is a violently spinning wind. It travels very fast across the land. The biggest tornadoes can pick up trees or houses and throw them through the air.

Hurricanes

Hurricanes are very large cyclones. Every year, the terrible winds and rain from hurricanes cause huge problems in the southeastern United States. Hurricanes also create giant ocean waves. These waves create **floods**. The floods can cause as much damage as the winds.

Hurricane Andrew

This is a view from space of Hurricane Andrew over the Gulf of Mexico in 1992.

A hurricane will cause enormous damage to property.
▽

hurricane   tropical cyclone

Gritty winds

When the wind blows, it picks up sand and little pieces of dirt. The wind carries the **grit** as it blows against mountains, hillsides, and along the ground. The gritty winds can damage crops. They also cause **erosion** over time. A wind carrying sand will wear away a rock's surface.

Ruined crops

Every year farmers face the problem of weather damage to crops. The spinach field below was wiped out by a **hurricane** in 1999.

grit   small, rough grains, such as sand, dust, or tiny bits of rock

Sandy hills

Sand is created from weathered rock. In areas where there is a lot of sand, wind blows it into mounds. The mounds are named **sand dunes**. The biggest are found in deserts or along beaches. Even big sand dunes do not stand still. The wind moves them around.

Highest dunes

The world's highest sand dunes are taller than the Empire State Building They are 1526 feet (465 meters) high. The dunes are in Algeria in Africa.

◁ These massive sand dunes are in Namibia in Africa.

sand dune   hill made of drifting sand

People and Erosion

People do many things to change Earth. We **erode** our planet in different ways.

How people affect Earth

We use Earth to grow food and provide **energy**. The way we live on our planet has changed the land, the oceans, and the **atmosphere**.

Fatal landslides

In 1903, more than 70 people were killed in a coal-**mining** town in Canada. Too much mining inside a mountain there had made the ground unstable. Over 80 million tons of rock fell in a sudden **landslide**.

Oil rigs off the coast of Texas drill deep into the ocean floor. ▽

Polluting the air

When we burn fuel to make energy, we **pollute** the air. Every day factories and vehicles send out fumes that go into the air we breathe. These fumes can make people sick.

Eroding the land

Coal, oil, and metals are some of the things we dig out of the ground by mining. Mining can erode the ground. It can also pollute water supplies.

Traffic fumes

Cars and trucks, like the ones below, pollute the air. The gasoline they burn gives out poisonous fumes.

Pollution and trees

The **chemicals** that **pollute** the **atmosphere** are not just harmful to people. They also **erode** rock and kill trees.

Acid rain

Acid rain damages thousands of square miles of forest each year. This rain is produced when fumes from factories and cars mix with water in the air. When it rains, this water has harmful chemicals in it. Acid rain eats away at plants and can kill whole forests.

Farming in steps

Some farming helps to prevent **erosion**. Farmers in Asia build steps into the hillside, such as those below. The crops they plant bind the soil together. This helps to stop **landslides**.

This spruce forest in the Czech Republic has been destroyed by acid rain. ▽

Wild Words   acid rain   rain containing harmful chemicals

Vanishing forests

Forests once covered much of the land on Earth. Today there is much less forest. Everywhere, trees are being cut down so we can use the wood. Huge areas of forest have also been cleared for farming. When the trees are gone, many animals lose their natural **habitat**. The soil is soon eroded, too.

New forests
Today many foresters plant new trees, like those above, to replace ones they cut down.

habitat   place where a plant or animal naturally lives or grows

35

Dry land

During a drought, the land dries up and is easily **eroded**. Nothing can grow in dry, eroded soil like that shown below.

Combined impact

Sometimes natural causes and human **impact** combine to cause **erosion**. You can see this when a **drought** strikes an area that has been farmed too much.

Farms in the Dust Bowl were buried by huge dust storms that blew through the area. ▽

Dust Bowl

The Great **Plains** of the United States used to be natural grassland. In the early 1900s, farmers removed the grass and planted wheat. The soil became eroded from too much farming.

When a drought struck in the 1930s, the land became dry and dusty. High winds simply blew the soil away. The region became known as the "Dust Bowl."

Dry sea

The Aral Sea in Asia was once the fourth largest inland sea in the world. Much of its water has been used for farming. Large areas of the sea (above) have started to dry up.

plains   large areas of grassland with few trees

Crowded world

Every year, the **population** of Earth grows. More people means more **impact** on the **environment**.

More and more people are traveling to distant places for vacations. Many people traveling means there is more **pollution** from cars, airplanes, and buses. It also means changes for the wild places that people like to visit.

Tourist traffic

Heavy traffic in Yellowstone Park, Wyoming (below), causes pollution and threatens animal **habitats**.

Wild Words conservation action to keep things protected or prevent waste

Preserving wilderness

In many parts of the world, people have created parks and **conservation** areas to protect fragile **ecosystems**. Many of these places are beautiful areas. But if millions of people visit these places, they can destroy the habitat of wild animals. They can also **erode** the land.

Crowds of tourists come to photograph wild animals in the Ngorongoro Conservation Area in Tanzania in Africa.
▽

Underwater world

This is an aerial photograph of The Great Barrier **Reef** off the coast of Australia. It is an ocean ecosystem. Thousands of divers come to the reef every year. The reef has become damaged by divers.

ecosystem   living things and non-living things that form a group in nature

Looking to the Future

One of the most serious effects we are having on Earth is the way we are changing the **climate**.

Polluting the atmosphere

Carbon dioxide in the air traps the Sun's heat. The trapped heat keeps Earth warm and helps living things survive. But when we burn fuel for **energy**, we create more carbon dioxide than usual. The extra carbon dioxide traps even more heat. This is called global warming.

Global warming ▷
may melt huge
areas of ice.

Wild Words carbon dioxide gas in Earth's atmosphere that comes from burning fuels

The ozone layer

Something else is adding to global warming. Around Earth is a layer of **ozone**. The ozone layer protects us from the Sun's harmful rays. For years we have been using **chemicals** that damage the ozone layer. In some places, the ozone layer is so thin that there are holes in it.

What will happen?

Global warming may bring some huge changes. Summers might become very hot. There may be more **droughts**. Melting ice and snow may cause serious **floods** around the world.

Eroding habitat
With global warming the **habitats** of animals in the **Arctic** (above) and **Antarctic** are threatened.

ozone   gas in the atmosphere that protects Earth from the Sun's harmful rays

Renewing the world

Erosion is not always bad. It is often the way that Earth renews itself. Mountains are worn away. The small pieces of rock become soil. Soil is blown or washed away. It becomes **compressed** on the ocean floor to form new rock. **Volcanoes** create new mountains. This process is known as the rock cycle.

Volunteers work to repair the effects of erosion on a hillside. ▽

Fighting erosion

These **groins** have been built to stop erosion along the coastline.

Wild Words compressed squeezed together

Recycling for the future

People can also help Earth renew itself. **Recycling** paper means fewer trees need to be cut down. Recycling cans and bottles helps reduce garbage. If we use less **energy**, we save fuel. This cuts down on air **pollution**. These are all things we can do to fight harmful erosion of our planet.

People in Mexico City wear masks to protect themselves from air pollution. ▽

groin   wood or metal structure built out from the shore to stop erosion

Find Out More

Organizations

United States Geological Survey

The USGS is a federal organization for science about the Earth. Its scientists study rocks, landslides, volcanoes, earthquakes, and more.

The USGS carries out research, responds to emergencies and disasters, and gives out information.

To find out more, contact them at this address:

USGS National Center, 12201 Sunrise Valley Drive, Reston, VA 20192

Books

Hunter, Rebecca. *Discovering Geography: Weather*. Chicago: Raintree, 2003.

Morris, Neil. *Landscapes and People: Earth's Changing Mountains*. Chicago: Raintree, 2003.

Redmond, Jim and Ronda. *Nature on the Rampage: Landslides*. Chicago: Raintree, 2003.

World Wide Web

To find out more about landslides and erosion you can search the Internet. Use keywords like these:

- landslide +news +[date]
- "acid rain" +landslide
- erosion +forests
- effects +"global warming"

You can find your own keywords by using words from this book. The search tips opposite will help you find useful websites.

Search tips

There are billions of pages on the Internet. It can be difficult to find exactly what you are looking for. These tips will help you find useful websites more quickly:

- Know what you want to find out
- Use simple keywords.
- Use two to six keywords in a search.
- Only use names of people, places, or things.
- Put double quote marks around words that go together, for example "sand dune".

Where to look

Search engine

A search engine looks through millions of website pages. It lists all the sites that match the words in the search box. You will find the best matches are at the top of the list, on the first page.

Search directory

A person instead of a computer has sorted a search directory. You can search by keyword or subject and browse through the different sites. It is like looking through books on a library shelf.

Glossary

absorb soak up

acid rain rain containing harmful chemicals

Antarctica South Pole and the region around it

Arctic North Pole and the region around it

atmosphere layer of gases surrounding Earth and other planets

avalanche quickly falling mass of snow, ice, rocks, or mud

canyon deep, steep valley

carbon dioxide gas in Earth's atmosphere that comes from burning fuels

chemical substance, such as gasoline or paint, made by mixing or separating other substances

climate the usual, or average, weather of a place

compressed squeezed together

conservation action to keep things protected or prevent waste

crust outer solid surface of Earth

cyclone storm made by spinning winds

dissolve process by which solids go into a liquid, usually water

drought long period with severe lack of rainfall

earthquake shaking of part of Earth's surface

ecosystem living things and non-living things that form a group in nature

energy the ability to do work

environment conditions and natural world that surrounds us

erode slowly wear away

erosion wearing away by wind, water, ice, or other forces

erupt burst through the surface, as when lava, gases, and ash burst out of a volcano

expand get bigger

fault crack or fracture in Earth's crust

flood large amount of water that spreads over land

gas substance, such as oxygen, that has no fixed shape or size

glacier slow-moving river of ice

gorge narrow valley between hills or mountains

gravel mixture of sand and small stones

grit small, rough grains, such as sand, dust, or tiny bits of rock

groin wood or metal structure built out from the shore to stop erosion

habitat place where a plant or animal naturally lives or grows

hurricane tropical cyclone

impact effect of one thing on another

landslide downward movement of land that can carry whole hillsides away

lava melted rock that erupts from a volcano

limestone type of rock in which caves are common

mining   digging in the earth for minerals like coal or metal ores

nutrient   substance that helps things grow

ozone   gas in the atmosphere that protects Earth from the Sun's harmful rays

plains   large areas of grassland with few trees

plate   rigid sections of Earth's hard outer layers

pollute   make air, water, or land dirty

pollution   harmful things in air, in water, or on land

population   number of people

recycling   using things again to avoid waste; and processing things so they can be reused

reef   ridge of rock, coral, or sand in a body of water

rift valley   valley formed when a block of land slips down between faults

riverbed   channel occupied by a river

sand dune   hill made of drifting sand

shingle   mass of small rocks on the shore of an ocean or lake

starvation   extreme lack of food or death from hunger

tornado   violently spinning wind that moves across land

tropical   having to do with or coming from the tropics, which is the region of Earth either side of the equator

tsunami   huge ocean wave caused by an earthquake, landslide, or volcanic eruption

vegetation   living plants, including trees

volcano   opening in Earth's crust from which melted rock and hot gases escape

weathering   erosion of rocks or soil by the weather

Index